In The Aftermath

Alaina Hasse

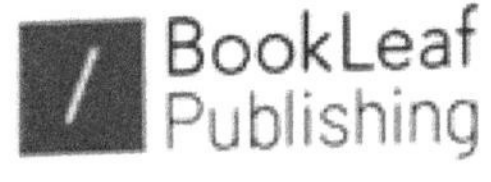

Presentation by *BookLeaf Publishing*

Web: www.bookleafpub.com

E-mail: info@bookleafpub.com

ISBN: 9789357210331

First edition 2022

DEDICATION

To my soul,

For never leaving.

To the people who love me,

For never giving up on me.

The Diagnosis

Swallowing in a splendor
This sadness that's selfish
Succumbed to the spell of my body
Take this sickness and make it yours
Vying for something to define you
And you finally got it

Bipolar

Are you there God?

I can't remember the last time I felt like the parts
of myself fit
Sighs, sights, and sirens
Everything has been set alight
Imposter syndrome or am I just a fraud?
The thought slaps me in the jaw and sends me
into solitude

Looking at myself in the mirror like she is my
loyal congregation
Seeking benedictions,
I can't bear myself
Ran out of blessings and prayers to save me
I wonder if the lord will still take me

What I am

We think what we become
We are what we eat
We become our transgressions
And perpetuate the abuse

The hurried harm and secret blows
The soothing nothings or empty promises
The blows always landing
The damage never healing

We become the things we once feared
Once recoiled and swore we would reclaim
We become and we perpetuate
The things that ruin us
And forget who we are

Skeletons

Stripped my skin of skin and sickly sense kicked
in
But I've been around these parts before
Shit or sugar
A taste in my mouth, it's sour
But I still can't tell which is which

Validation veneered but I am still looking for
some sense of purification
Sin sunk in and stained my God within
The ghost of myself still chases blessings

Left in a rut, I'm not a runner
Constant contradictions
I don't trust these bones within me
Marrow with no merit, no color
I am no better than the skeletons that hang in the
back of my closet

Handprints and bruises riddle themselves across
my body
And I wonder
If they are mine
Or yours

The Beach

It's the sand and the sadness
The way the ocean never really can shake you
free from either
Just coating you in another cloak of shame
And you can never wash these things away

It's the welling and the water
The way it has you pulled completely under
Now you're learning to breathe all over again
All by yourself

Slashed and ripped gills
Side of neck, center of chest
But water still fills your lungs
Flexing and pumping, you choke on it all
through you

It's the sand and the sadness
The way the ocean can leer and loom over you
Fish dance with ghost
And you're not sure why but you know the steps
too

You come out of the water
Cloaked but not cleansed

You'll never be able to sink yourself beneath her
So she haunts you

The Toilet Bowl

Tooth and nail
It's sink or swim
Vendor of my bones and savior of my cheek
Down to the brittle and braille
Hematoma's growing or maybe it's just a bad
dream
I went looking for parts of myself in the toilet
again

I forgot nothing good comes up

Nihility

I am bleak, I am barren, and I am trying
And I don't know how or when I got to this
point
How I got to be this thing
Or when I turned to poison

I am bleak, I am barren, and I am trying
I would rip the skin off my back and give it
away if I could
And I wish I could
I wish I could pull myself away from myself
Pull her away at the seams and leave her in a
heap in a pile on the floor at my feet

I want to run away from myself
There must be something wrong with me
I am in a constant war
A never ending and fatal fight with myself
Caught somewhere between alive and a ghost
I just can't tell which

I have worked myself so hard my bones are now
ground to dust
And I am just waiting for the wind to come and
fucking take me

My veins and arteries sucked dry of their blood
And my marrow, so meek
I am wishing to breathe myself into nihility

That's non-existence
It is nothing if you don't know
My heart keeps beating and I keep breathing,
they're the only thing that keeps me alive
So why am I wishing for the one thing that
keeps me going to cause me to fucking
disappear

I don't know
I don't know
I just don't fucking know what I'm supposed to
do with myself
Or how I'm supposed to handle myself
When I'm too much for everybody else around
me

And yes, that includes me
My name is at the top of that list
Alaina knows my weaknesses
She knows what buttons to push and pull
The ones that I don't fuck with

She opens up my Bermuda box
Tucked away in my attic of a mind
She tells the ghosts to float through me

In my stick, stone, hollow bird bone body

Alaina
When will you stop breaking yourself down?
Nobody seems to understand and maybe that's
why you break and you break
A weight on your shoulders, a waiting game
Until it all comes down and topples to crush you

No one can see behind your looking glass eyes
into your wonderland mind
That really is no wonderland at all
It's a dark place

And nobody knows about the blood in your
veins and how it boils towards suicide
You think about the one, two, three, four or five
Or whoever knows how many times she tried
The one time she tried
The gunshot to heart
The gunshot to head
The gunshot to heart or head, I can't remember
which
The one who drowned in alcohol

I know what it's like to struggle from the within
to stay alive
My sick and poisoned bones

The toxicity I exude is going to burn right
through them
The toxicity I am is going to burn right through
Me

Frog

I am a frog set to boil
Wading in wait
Temperature rising
Water spits before she howls
And soon I will be screeching too

Raspy croaks and throaty trills
I don't even notice until it's too late
Before a hand stretches out and turns the flame
to high

I am a predator no more than I am prey
I hunt myself

The Muddle

I am stuck in the mud or a puddle
I am somewhere in the middle
It's walking a tightrope between feeling alive
and suicidal
And there's a buzzing in my brain

One so loud I can feel it in my ears
I am cicadas in full bloom
Screeching until I am only carcass
I don't realize I am stuck in this pattern
Trapped in this cycle
Until I start to scream again

No longer cicada, I am just sick
Each time I ask for help it turns into a scream
I am holding on to the shell of myself until she
decides it is time to give up
Only to do it all again

And I'm stuck
Somewhere in the middle of the mud and in the
puddle
In a cycle that has a chokehold on me
Do I have the gaul to break it?

So I sit in my puddle
In the mud and in the middle
On the tightrope at the center
And I wonder

Me

Feeding my body nothing once again
Full off of empty
And empty off of full
My bones operate better when there's a hunger
inside me

Swallowing air and espresso
Water and pain
I am filling up on mornings and getting high off
the afternoons
Come evening I've shed any hunger entirely

And I'm floating
Pixie dream girl out to play
Hardly pretty, but entirely
Manic

Maps

Yesterday you felt like you may have been down
Or at least on you way

But today you feel
All the way
Up

So far and so high

Your anchor has lifted you off the ground
How many other different direction will you go
in

Until you stop

Body of Christ

Lately I have been seeking absolution for this
body of mine
This body that has never known a church
Had to create one inside myself and relinquish
all that doubt
Stripping my sins of their sins
I want to wipe my slate clean

What was left at the end was the tender remains
of my shredded and shrunken soul
The fragments of grace that tried to save face
I have never spoken to God or Jesus
Always felt closer to Judas
We both had a habit of turning on people
Mine just happens to be myself

Gut

I think I'm doing it again but I don't mean to
I think it's because of the way air feels so
familiar in my gut
I'm full of sanctioned and practiced breaths
Controlling my breathing and practicing a
straight face

I can't make it seem like something is wrong
My belly is full off this feeling
And I don't have room for much else
I think it's because of the way the feeling comes
back, as it always does

Maybe it's what's turned my hums to hymns and
before I know it
I have a throat full of gospel but nothing to do
with God
I think it's because of the way a body never
forgets
It falls back into pattern
A sick syncopate, a symphony of sadness
Can you hear it?

Marked arms and marked legs
The bruises that stayed and the ones that left

And now skin and bone will never forget the
way it feels when blows land
The quota is always up for questioning
At which point do I give in instead of defend?

Tooth and nail, I hold no bar
I can't apologize for my ways of self protection
I'm afraid of so much now and it is myself on
the top of the list
I think it's because of the hollow
The way I'm so used to empty
It's the only way I have ever light and ever since
I could remember
I have wanted to be skinny

So, it's the same thing, right?
I can't fit in the palms of hands, not in the sides
of cheeks, or in the back of jaws
But
I'm constantly shrinking, trying to make myself
smaller
I think I'm doing it again and I don't mean to
Starving myself of everything and I have control
of nothing
So I crave it

Do I know who is running the show now?
I can't say that I do
And I think that's why I'm doing it again

But I don't mean to

Versus

And sometimes it feels like it is everyone
against me
Everything against me
I am both the rage and the machine
It is me against me
I versus I
And neither of us are going to win

Out of Body

It happened to me again today
My head rolled off my body in a fashion you
could call violent
Bursted off my shoulders and left the stump of
my neck exposed
The stump that I am all too familiar with
because I am constantly slipping outside of
myself

Spilling out of my fingertips and toes
Any effort to get away from these godforsaken
bones
And I think I'm ready to talk about it
Maybe I can start with forgiveness

I am a forest full of guilt
My tired eyes have tried their best
They are now sunken as my sadness has fully
flourished
And this feeling fixes itself inside me

Treading Water

I'm tired
I'm tired and I'm treading water
I've been treading water and I don't want to
tread this water anymore
I'm tired

I've been trying to keep myself afloat for longer
than I can remember
Legs kicking, arms swirling, limbs constantly
moving
The lactic acid has grown too strong for my
body to bear
Tendons and muscles begin to tear and the rest
of me rips through me

It's the parts of me I've tried to drown
And now I'm treading my own water
The sear of myself has now passed the muscle
and tendons
It's time to get down to bone

Lactic and leeching
I can feel myself slipping and the memories all
sweeping

I'm treading water inside my own chest and I can
barely breathe
I am a fish out of water, a girl with cut gills
Nobody knows how hard those cuts were
Or the rest of the ones I couldn't quite make

I'm kicking and flailing now
I'm treading water in the deepest parts of me
When did my body turn into a dark empty sea,
I know there have been stars and galaxies that
once were born all across me
Hematomas looked like constellations
I was full of handmade stars
Am I a cosmic being now because I know what
it's like to be an undiscovered comet?

Hues of blues and painful purples too
I can't tell you what its like to be beautiful
I can only tell you
What it's like to be broken

Ideations

I'm used to back burners
The quiet corner with a silent sear
The scent of myself - scorched

I'm used to being pulled under
Head above nothing but I still can't tell if my
feet are off the ground
Is it an anchor in my heart or wings?
Am I flying or am I falling?

I feel like I can almost reach it
It's the sea grabbing at me this time
And she is hungry
She keeps beckoning for me to come and get lost
in it's reach

Or maybe this time,
I am sizing up traffic and red lights
Playing footsie with my gas pedal
What's going to happen next?

Sour Ground

Bones full and blistered
Marrow seeping out as I burn holes in myself
Femur now flute
Air whistles through my hollow and stiff body
Crooked mouth opens and my words turn to
wind
I am simply sour ground
Nothing can grow here

The Girl Or The Globe

The bones slipped out the back and through the
seam
Zipping up my skin as they leave
My soul shook awake at the unsteady silence of
her house,
Of Me
Body barracking away the pain and guilt like
Frankenstein's monster

Waiting for the storm to come and revive me
I open up my mouth and nothing comes out
except for a wild pour of madness
It falls from my mouth in a bloody rain as the
words come squirming out of me
And no one can hear my cries for help

It's been so long since I ground my bones into
the dust they are now
No wind showed up to take me
To take the little pieces of me that my body let
slip away
Maybe I should ask for the dustpan, maybe I
need to clean up the after of myself

Fingerprints taint all the surfaces I touch

Grimy gold flakes leave rust behind as the world
decays with my passing
But my body's most loyal companion,
My depression - she has never left me
Maybe I can just blame global warming for my
constant moods changing

Glory?

I'm afraid
There's a fear of falling and failing with each
step that I take
My heart beats in my chest and I can feel her in
my ears
I can taste the sour smell of defeat on my lips as
I open up my mouth to ask for absolution
Somewhere deep inside myself I feel something
welling

It's buzzing and it rushes all through me
Filling my lungs and fracturing my fear
Taste full of new buds and my tongue has
become alert again
Heart shifts back into place and gear
As I hear this newfound glory
Grace and hope now deciding they will choose
me

My mouth full of grit
I am stumbling over tongue
I keep myself silent, so quiet
Afraid to open my mouth
Afraid that out spite or fear
I will reject them

A Vigil

Look in the mirror and want to say Jesus
But what comes out is Judas
And I can't remember the first time I turned my
back on myself
Forgive me of my sins
I need something to temper this self doubt

Maria,
It's been a while since we spoke last
But you're the only church that I've been to
The way we each packed something away in our
suitcases
Yours was God and mine was bruises
Hematoma hills and bloody noses that made me
feel like I was the body of Christ

The way teeth felt hollow
Like jumpers on the edge of a ledge
Waiting to make their leap but roots too seeded
Souls tethered down further than bite can sink
It's ascension, but not in the way that you think

It's the way the guilt can barrack and buckle
down
Hypomania and dry shampoo

Drowning in the sea and the sand or the sadness
But none of them can save me

Take a deep breath
Heart beating in a lump
Thumping each beat up my throat and out my
chest
Bipolar body
Who will I be today?

Quavered, cracked, and caved
Let me put on a brave face for you
Its the gully and the gaul the way a mind can
make me resent me
My body a vestigial organ

I mean
I meant to say a vigil of an organism
One that's tongue tied and twisted
Kin came out as cancer and melanoma crept
under my grandfathers beautiful brown skin
And I wonder what will come for me next

Cradle me in it's covers and which fight will I
win
Look in the mirror and meant to say Judas
But it comes out as Jesus
I found my own God in myself
And I thank her for saving me